Creating Meaningful Funeral

Ceremonies

A Guide for Families

REVISED EDITION

ALAN D. WOLFELT, PH.D.

Also by Alan D. Wolfelt, Ph.D.:

Funeral Home Customer Service A-Z:
Creating Exceptional Experiences for Today's Families

The Journey Through Grief: Reflections on Healing

Healing the Bereaved Child: Grief Gardening, Growth

Through Grief and Other Touchstones for Caregivers

Healing Your Grieving Heart: 100 Practical Ideas

Understanding Your Grief: Ten Essential Touchstones
for Finding Hope and Healing Your Heart

Companion Press is dedicated to the education and support of both the bereaved
and bereavement caregivers. We believe that those who companion the bereaved
by walking with them as they journey in grief have a wondrous opportunity: to
help others embrace and grow through grief—and to lead fuller, more deeply-lived
lives themselves because of this important ministry.

Companion Press is a division of the Center for Loss and Life Transition,
located in Fort Collins, Colorado.

Companion
P R E S S

For ordering information, write or call:
Companion Press
a division of
The Center for Loss and Life Transition
3735 Broken Bow Road
Fort Collins, CO 80526
(970) 226-6050
www.centerforloss.com

Creating Meaningful Funeral

Ceremonies

A Guide for Families
REVISED EDITION

ALAN D. WOLFELT, PH.D.

Companion
PRESS

An imprint of the Center for Loss and Life Transition

Companion Press is an imprint of the Center for Loss and Life Transition,

3735 Broken Bow Road, Fort Collins, Colorado 80526.

Manufactured in the Unites States of America

16 15 14 13 12 11   5 4 3 2 1

ISBN: 978-1-879651-20-3

To my father; Don Wolfelt, who modeled the importance of gathering for family ceremonies. Perhaps unknowingly, he taught me the value of coming together among friends and family to acknowledge important life events, including funerals that acknowledged a death while remembering a life. Thanks, Dad, for helping me recognize that when words are inadequate, create a meaningful ceremony. My hope is that your influence will live on in me through my writings, my teachings, and my daily living.

Contents

Preface 9
Introduction 11
Planning a Funeral is a Privilege 12
Making the Initial Decisions.................................... 13
  • Having a Family Meeting................................... 13
  • Choosing a Funeral Home 13
  • Working with Your Funeral Director 15
  • The Arrangement Conference with Your Funeral Director...... 16
  • Some Information Your Funeral Director
    Will Need (worksheet) 17
  • Choosing Someone to Lead the Ceremony 19
  • What Kind of Service Will You Have?................. 20
  • General Service Types 21
  • What Will Happen to the Body.......................... 25
  • Combination of Service Choices and Disposition Choices 27
  • Financial Considerations 28
Planning a Meaningful Funeral Ceremony 31
  • The Elements of Funeral Ceremonies................. 31
    - The Visitation.. 31
    - The Service 32
        The Eulogy.. 32
        Music 37
        Memories 37
        Symbols.. 39
    - The Procession 41
    - The Committal Service 41
    - The Gathering or Reception............................ 42
  • Personalizing This Funeral Service (worksheet) 44
  • Some Ideas for Personalizing a Funeral Service.......... 47
Glossary of Funeral Terms 49
Afterwords: Understanding Grief............................ 51
Ongoing Ways of Remembering and Honoring the Life............ 59
A Final Word... 63
Recommended Readings...................................... 65
Organizations for Mourners 67
Funeral Planning Summary (worksheet)................... 69
About the Author.. 75

Preface

This book is one small effort to help mourners in the days just before and after a death. If you are reading it, I suspect someone in your family is either dying or has just died. You may be feeling numb and overwhelmed with all the details that must be attended to. You may not know what you are expected to do. You may even be questioning the need to have a funeral.

Most of us are never really "prepared" for the death of someone we have given love to and received love from. And right now you are bereaved, which literally means, "to be torn apart" and "to have special needs." Right now I encourage you to take a deep breath and try to breathe in and out slowly. You are not alone. This resource and many caring people (family, friends, funeral directors, clergy) are ready to help you plan and carry out a funeral ceremony that will be meaningful to you, your family, and friends.

"A funeral ritual encourages the heart to open to its grief as well as to trust in what exists beyond the senses."
— Stephen Levine

You'll note that throughout this book I encourage you to work with a funeral home in the coming days. Unlike other texts on funeral planning, this is not a "do it yourself" manual. I wholeheartedly encourage you to take charge of planning this funeral, of making it a personalized, fitting tribute to the person who died. I do not, however, advocate handling all the details of death and burial yourself. Those are best overseen by the funeral home staff, who are experienced in these matters and familiar with the customs, legal issues and resources in your community. Let them handle the behind-the-scenes details while you spend your time and energy creating a well-planned, inclusive, personalized funeral ceremony that will honor and remember the person who died.

This book has been designed in an easy-to-scan format that includes space for you to jot down your ideas as well as details such as names and phone numbers. If you read through or skim the whole book, stopping to make notes along the way, it will become your funeral planning notebook—a place to store all the information that will be required of you in the coming days.

Sometimes, caring funeral directors are also very willing and able to assist you in creating a meaningful, personalized funeral experience. Remember, the making of an excellent funeral requires what I like to call your intentional attention!

This guide is not meant to be a reference book that takes up space on a shelf. Rather, it is a tool to use at the time of the death of someone you love. Make this resource work for your unique needs. Write notes to yourself in the spaces provided and in the margins. Skip sections that don't apply to you. And remember—you and your family are the experts at creating a funeral ceremony that will best meet your needs and reflect your values.

Cordially,

Alan D. Wolfelt

Alan D. Wolfelt, Ph.D.
Director, Center for Loss and Life Transition
May 2011

The Funeral Planning Summary Worksheet at the back of this book gives you a single spot to sum up all the choices you'll make and information you'll need for this funeral. If you don't have time to read or skim the entire book, just turn to p. 69 and, together with your family, begin filling out this worksheet.

Introduction

As you enter into the planning process, you may find it helpful to remind yourself why we have funerals.

For thousands of years, funerals have been a means of expressing our beliefs, thoughts and feelings about the death of someone we love.

"Do not separate yourself from community."
— Hillel

The funeral ceremony:

• helps us acknowledge that someone we love has died.

• allows us to say hello on the pathway to goodbye.

• helps us remember the person who died and encourages us to share those memories with others.

• offers a time and place for us to talk about the life and death of the person who died.

• provides a social support system for us and other friends and family members.

• allows us to search for the meaning of life and death.

• offers continuity and hope for the living.

• helps us take our grief and convert it to mourning.

One of the most important gifts of planning a meaningful funeral is that it helps you and your family to focus your thoughts and feelings on something positive. The funeral encourages you to think about the person who has died and to explore the meaning of her life and the ways in which she touched the lives of others.

The remembering, deciding, and reflecting that takes place in the planning of the service are often an important part of the process of grief and mourning. And ultimately, this process of contemplation and discovery creates a memorable and moving funeral experience for all who attend.

Grief or mourning?

As you plan this funeral, keep in mind the important difference between grief and mourning. Grief is the internal thoughts and feelings we all have when someone we love dies. Mourning, on the other hand, is the outward expression of those thoughts and feelings. It is through mourning that we integrate life losses into our lives. Personalized, well-thought-out funeral ceremonies help us mourn. And so, funerals help us begin to heal.

Understanding the six needs of mourning

As people in mourning, we need to have six needs met if we are to integrate loss into our lives:

Need 1. Acknowledge the reality of the death.
Need 2. Embrace the pain of the loss.
Need 3. Remember the person who died.
Need 4. Develop a new self-identity.
Need 5. Search for meaning.
Need 6. Continue to receive support from others.

While we cannot fully meet all of these needs in one fell swoop, the funeral ceremony and the funeral planning process will begin to "dose" you in the six needs of mourning. The funeral is about a "good beginning" to your authentic mourning.

For a more detailed discussion of the six needs of mourning, please see p. 54 of this text.

> *"The funeral process establishes significance. That is what the funeral is for and that is the value of the funeral."*
> — Doug Manning

Planning a Funeral is a Privilege

As you consider the funeral, try to remember that planning the funeral of someone you love is not a burden, but a privilege. Think of the funeral as a gift to the person who died. It is your chance to think about and express the value of the life that was lived. It is also your chance to say hello on the pathway to goodbye!

This is not to deny your need to mourn and to embrace painful feelings of grief in the coming days. You may feel deep sadness as you plan this funeral and begin to acknowledge the reality of the death. But when all is said and done, you will also feel deep satisfaction that you have helped plan a meaningful tribute to someone who has meant a lot to you.

> *"When we pause to discover the sacredness in life and death through the use of ceremony, we are reborn, renewed, transformed."*
> — Alan Wolfelt

Making The Initial Decisions

Having A Family Meeting

It is often helpful to have a private family meeting before going in to see the funeral director. This can be a time for expressing your grief together as well as a time for some initial decision-making.

Find a place free of interruptions and sit down together. You might use this planning guide to discuss the different types of services available to your family. Try as best you can to include everyone in the discussion. No one should feel left out.

Also remember that even though you as family members are feeling drained, now is a time to strive for family unity. Try to pull together and consider the needs of all family members and friends. Don't always choose the "easy" things; instead, plan to include the elements of funeral ceremonies that will ultimately help all of you reconcile yourself to this death.

As you begin to discuss service options, you may be faced with the conflict of honoring the wishes of the person who has died as well as your own wishes as survivors. While it is natural to want to meet the requests of the person who died, do consider changes or embellishments that will be helpful to your family. Remember—funerals are for the living and if you have a need, now is the time to express it.

"A man's dying is more the survivors' affair than his own."
— Thomas Mann

Choosing a Funeral Home

The funeral home and its staff play a critical role in the planning and carrying out of a meaningful funeral. After all, they are the people with training and expertise and you will rely on them in the next several days. Their advice, their compassion, their attention to detail and their willingness to personalize THIS ceremony will greatly influence the funeral you end up with.

There are differences among funeral homes. Some are very good at helping families and some aren't so good. Some are open to new ideas and to adding unique, personalized touches in honor of the person who died—and some aren't.

So, which funeral home will you use? Because you probably have so little time (and even less energy) right now, it's unreasonable to expect you to visit and interview several funeral homes before selecting one. (If you have the time and energy, by all means, do.) But you can read over and consider the following list of questions before deciding. You can also phone local friends, family, neighbors, and clergy and ask for their recommendations.

- What is the reputation of this funeral home? Have you talked with other families who have used their services? What do they have to say?

- Which funeral home has your family used in the past? Did you have a meaningful experience and receive good service and respect from the staff? Does the funeral home have a true commitment to the families it serves?

- Do you already know someone on the staff at a funeral home? If so, could he or she help ensure that you will receive excellent service?

- Where is the funeral home located? Is it in a convenient location? What is the facility like? Is it clean and well-kept? Is the decor a good match for the tastes of your family? (If you are using another location for the visitation and ceremony, such as a church, these questions may not apply to you.)

- Does the funeral home provide services beyond the funeral itself? Do they provide grief education and support materials? Can the funeral home refer you and your family for additional services you might want and need?

- Is the funeral home willing to openly discuss costs? Do they provide itemized or package pricing? Can they provide you with a description of the services you will receive? (Note that the Federal Trade Commission requires that all funeral homes provide itemized pricing information on a general price list so that customers can compare prices. Do not hesitate to ask to review the funeral home's general price list and ask them to clarify any questions you may have.)

Keep in mind that the funeral you have is essentially a statement your family makes to the community at large: "Someone precious to us has died. We are in grief and invite you to join us in remembering a life and supporting each other." Ask yourself: Will this funeral home help me create a service unique to our needs and values?

Notes on local funeral homes (jot down phone numbers, too)

_____

_____

_____

_____

_____

Working With Your Funeral Director

Every bit as important as the funeral home you choose is the specific funeral director who will help you with the arrangements and service details.

What makes an excellent funeral director? He or she should be able to provide you the information, knowledge and counsel you need to plan a funeral that will meet your family's needs. The funeral director you work with should also be genuine, warm, and caring. He or she should be capable of helping facilitate (which literally means "to make easier") a meaningful ceremony for you and your family.

An excellent funeral director will have empathy for how difficult and draining arranging a funeral can be for you and your family. It is here that his or her genuine caring and sensitivity should shine through.

Does the funeral director listen and respect your unique needs? Does he or she encourage you to be creative and offer suggestions on how to personalize the service? Does the funeral director have the desire and ability to connect with you and your family? Is he or she patient and willing to take as much time as you need to plan and carry out a meaningful service?

If you so choose, will the funeral director allow you to help care for the body of the person you have loved? Some families, for example, take great comfort in dressing the body or doing the make-up or fixing the hair. If this is important to you, ask the funeral director if this is possible. If that is not something you care to do, that is okay, too.

If you are certain that the funeral director is a sincere, knowledgeable and compassionate person who has your family's best interests in mind, then you need look no further. On the other hand, if you are not comfortable working with this particular funeral director, do not hesitate to ask for someone else; many funeral homes have two or three funeral directors on staff. If you have a preference for working with a female or a male funeral director, let this be known to the funeral home. Their job is to help meet your expectations and exceed them whenever possible.

If time allows, visit the funeral home and talk to the director you will be working with. Remember—it is your choice and it is an important one! Don't settle; find a funeral director and funeral home that truly want to help you and your family. Treat your funeral director with respect and he or she will likely respond in kind. However, while you should maintain respect and express gratitude for the help you receive, remember to insist that the needs and values of your family are the most important.

Your Funeral Director

Name_____

Funeral Home_____

Phone number_____ Cell phone number_____

Notes

_____

_____

_____

_____

The Arrangement Conference with Your Funeral Director

You may have already scheduled a time to meet with your funeral director to help you plan the funeral. This meeting is called the "arrangement conference." During the arrangement conference, the funeral director will gather important information about the person who died and help you make funeral choices. Reading this resource and filling in some of the blanks before the arrangement conference will help you in both arranging for and carrying out a purposeful funeral.

What to Bring to the Arrangement Conference

_____ A photo for the obituary (although not all newspapers will print photos). Something fairly recent is most appropriate; a clear "head and shoulders" shot is best, though your newspaper can crop or enlarge almost any photo. The photo can be color or black and white.

_____ Discharge papers if the person who died was a veteran and you would like veteran's honors at the funeral.

_____ Clothing for the person who died. Often families choose a nice suit for a man or a nice dress for a woman, though anything that reflects the tastes and personality of the person who died is appropriate. Include undergarments and a pair of socks. Shoes are not needed but are sometimes placed alongside the body. Ask your funeral director for advice if you're unsure about clothing.

_____ Your desire to create a personalized, meaningful ceremony! If you and your family come to the arrangement conference with a true desire to plan a loving tribute to the person who died, you are bringing the most important thing of all.

_____ Background information (see p. 17-18).

Some Information Your Funeral Director Will Need

Following is some of the information your funeral director will need when you meet with him to arrange the funeral. Much of the personal data (such as social security number and place of birth) are required by law for the death certificate. Your funeral director will use some of the other information to submit the obituary to the newspapers of your choice. Jotting down some of the answers now may help you feel more prepared for the arrangement conference.

IMPORTANT: Did the person who died prearrange his or her funeral? If yes, please locate his or her instructions. Your funeral director may also be able to help you locate them.

Name of the person who died

_____

First (full)   Middle   Last

Nickname (sometimes used in the obituary and the service)_____

Date of birth_____ Place of birth_____

Age at death_____ Date of death_____ Place of death_____

Cause or description of death_____

Social Security number (in Canada, Social Insurance Number)

_____

Was the person who died a veteran?   _____ yes_____ no

If yes, which branch of the armed services and when?_____
(Please bring his or her discharge papers if you can.)

Father's name_____

Mother's name (inc. maiden name)_____

Siblings' names _____

Married to (inc. maiden name)_____ When_____ Where_____

Children's names and places of residence_____

_____

How many grandchildren?__ Great-grandchildren?__ Great-great grandchildren?___

Preceded in death by _____

_____

Survived by _____

_____

Has lived in _____ since _____

Former place(s) of residence _____

Education _____

Employment _____

Civic/church involvement _____

_____

Honors _____

_____

Will the body be buried or cremated? _____

If buried, where? (include cemetery and plot details if you have them _____

_____

If cremated, what will be done with the remains? _____

Memorials/donations _____

Newspapers in which you'd like the obituary to appear (Don't forget out-of-town
newspapers): _____

_____

_____

Notes _____

_____

_____

Choosing Someone to Lead the Ceremony

The person who leads the funeral service is usually the single most influential person in this process. So, you want to be sure that this person is open to meeting your unique family's needs and to personalizing the ceremony as much as possible.

Experienced funeral leaders (typically clergy) often have certain ways of doing things and may feel constrained in their ability to go outside the bounds of their liturgical traditions. Often, the faith's prayerbook and church rules and traditions dictate service options. However, there are some excellent clergy who will work with you to help you achieve a wonderfully personalized ceremony that is still in keeping with the religion's traditions.

If you or the person who died attended a church or other place of worship, a clergyperson from this church will likely be the logical choice to lead the funeral ceremony you are planning. Expressing your family's faith through a religious service at the time of a death is both fitting and healing.

But a religious service doesn't need to be an impersonal, cookie-cutter service straight out of the prayerbook. Talk to your clergyperson about appropriate ways of personalizing the ceremony. Perhaps special readings and music can be added. Maybe a DVD full of important memories can be shown. I urge both you and your clergyperson to be creative and free-thinking as you plan a fitting final tribute to the unique person who died.

Families often tell me that the eulogy (also called the remembrance or homily) was the most meaningful part of the funeral ceremony they held—but only if the eulogy was personalized. Keep in mind that the eulogy doesn't have to be delivered by the person leading the service. Only if your clergyperson knows your family well and can speak personally about the person who died is this appropriate. If the clergyperson didn't know the person who died, it's much more meaningful to have a family member or friend of the family give the eulogy. Or you might ask several people to speak. (For more on eulogies, see p. 32.)

If your family or the person who died are not members of a church or other place of worship, however, you may feel no connection to a certain clergyperson or body of faith. When this is the case, consider asking a family member, friend of the family, funeral director or other person with good public speaking skills to lead the ceremony. In fact, this is a growing trend across North America. Virtually anybody can be a funeral facilitator. No experience is necessary—just a desire to honor the person who died.

If you choose to go this route, you can create your own service by choosing fitting readings (religious or non-religious) and music. Be sure to include a eulogy or time of remembrance (see p. 32). I would also encourage you to use as many of the other elements of funeral ceremony as possible, such as the visitation, the procession, the committal, etc. (see p. 31.) These will help lend structure and ultimately give meaning to the service you hold.

Another option today is hiring a "celebrant" to lead the service. The celebrant movement is fairly new in the U.S. Celebrants create ceremonies to acknowledge life transitions, including funerals. There are approximately 400 "life cycle celebrants" in the U.S. today. Celebrants work with the family to choose music, readings, and words to honor their loved one's life. If you do choose to hire a celebrant, make sure he or she is a good fit for the needs of your family. Most celebrants are dedicated to what they do and will work with you to create a meaningful funeral.

If you don't have someone in mind to lead this funeral, talk to your funeral director. They should have a list of compassionate people who they have seen do an excellent job of helping families create meaningful funerals. Before reviewing this list with your funeral director, however, be sure to emphasize what kind of service you would like to have. Some funeral facilitators will only be comfortable with certain kinds of services.

What Kind of Service Will You Have?

You can choose from a variety of funeral service types and formats. Some people think that funerals must conform to "traditional" ways. Yet, let me remind you that there is no one right way to have a funeral. Just as grief has many dimensions and is experienced in different ways by different people, funerals will be unique also. A funeral should simply "fit" the person who died and the family and friends who survive him. Don't be afraid to be creative; this is a time for the honest expression of your most heartfelt values. Feel free to honor the person who died without following rigid rules or being worried about "what's usually done."

Before planning the specifics of the funeral, you may find it helpful to consider the goals of the service you will hold. You may even want to write them down.

For example, as we plan this funeral we will strive to:

1. Create a ceremony that remembers how John's life has impacted our lives.

2. Give testimony to John's faith life.

3. Ensure that John's body is treated respectfully.

4. Provide ourselves with a time and place to support each other at this difficult time.

5. Provide meaningful references to John's life through stories, music, pictures, and words that evoke a connection to John, an appreciation for his life, and an acknowledgement of his death.

The choices you make about the type of service you make will all originate from these goals.

Once you have defined the goals you would like to accomplish with this particular funeral, you can then ask yourself: How do we accomplish these overall goals? How do we turn these general goals into a meaningful service? Before we go on, try brainstorming a list of the general goals you want to meet through this service.

Goals for this funeral ceremony

_____

_____

_____

_____

_____

General Service Types

The following is a brief, broad description of different service types used throughout North America. As you read the general descriptions, keep in mind the type of service that will best meet the needs of your unique family after the death of this unique person. Again, there is no one right funeral type. With changes in culture and customs, an increasing number of North Americans are making use of various aspects of ceremony that don't always fit within the following broad definitions. Moreover, the following categories are not mutually exclusive. In practice, many real-life funerals blur the lines. The specific "type" of service you have is not as important as how it helps you, your family, and your friends find meaning and purpose at this time in your life.

Traditional Funeral Service

A service held in the presence of the body, with either an open or closed casket. A member of the clergy usually officiates and the service is held within two or three days of the death. A visitation period often precedes the funeral. The service is usually held in a church or funeral home chapel. There is usually a religious message to the ceremony. The specific denomination's (Protestant, Catholic, etc.) book of worship determines specific elements of ritual used. The ceremony itself often consists of scripture readings, prayers, a eulogy, sometimes a sermon, usually interspersed with music and hymns. After the funeral there may be a procession to the gravesite or crematory chapel, where a brief committal service concludes the ceremony. When planning the funeral, the family decides whether the service will be public or private.

Memorial Service

A memorial service is a service held without the body present (though the cremated remains may be present in an urn). Disposition of the body may take place either before or after the service. Some memorial services are not held until weeks or months after the death. The service may be religious or non-religious. There are many different types of memorial services and they may be held in funeral homes, churches, private homes, community rooms or outdoors.

A memorial service may be held instead of a funeral, or in addition to it. For example, you might have a funeral in the town where a person lived most of her life and ultimately died, and a memorial service at a later time in the community where she was raised. As with a more traditional funeral service, the final form of disposition of the body may be either earth burial or cremation.

Affirmation or Celebration of Life Service

More and more today terms such as these are being used to describe funeral services. Such services vary widely in content and format, but they tend to be more personalized and more upbeat. The body may or may not be present. They can be religious or non-religious and they can be held almost anywhere. The only rule seems to be that no rules apply!

However, I urge you to not think of this funeral as a party. There is a trend today to celebrate someone's life, rather than acknowledge his or her death, at the funeral. More and more people are saying things like: "When I die, just get rid of me...no muss, no fuss. Maybe you can throw a party, but I sure don't want a funeral!" Many of us now believe that having fun, feeling joy (and surprise), and being entertained are what having an experience is all about. And regrettably, we've transferred this idea onto funerals. Some of us in today's modern society have forgotten that the purpose of a funeral is to mourn, to actively and outwardly embrace the death of someone we love.

We have confused honoring with celebration and celebration with partying. Webster defines party as "a gathering for social entertainment." Is this what you want for the funeral of your loved one? Most likely, you answered no. What reinforces this desire for fun, entertainment, and celebration is that mourning is painful and not something we want to readily sign up to do. It is easier to celebrate than to express the emotions of sadness and hurt. It's often our desire, when we are hurting, to "be strong" and "get over it" quickly. Others tell us to "carry on," "keep your chin up," and remind us that the person who died is "in a better place."

Yet this urge to keep things light and move on quickly denies the authentic suffering of the soul, whereas meaningful funerals invite an encounter with the mystery. Historically, funerals honored the need for downward movement—going through grief rather than around it. Authentic mourning demands that we slow down, befriend dark emotions, and seek and accept support. Doing so helps place the loss in a larger, transcendent realm of meaning. The more we try to "party" in the face of loss, the more we end up grieving and not mourning. Grief is an internal response to loss, where mourning is an outward expression of grief, a shared, social response to loss.

The major purpose of a meaningful ceremony is to begin to convert grief into mourning in the loving and supportive company of others who share our grief. Of course, this is not to say that a meaningful funeral should be totally devoid of celebration and laughter. Funny anecdotes about the person who died and jokes delivered during the eulogy are often a welcome and necessary part of the experience. When someone loved dies, we feel many feelings, including the bittersweet joy of reliving favorite memories. Sharing those memories is part of the journey, too—one that gives us moments of relief even as we dose ourselves with the necessary sadness. As you plan your funeral, always remember those important words, "blessed are those who mourn." This doesn't mean "blessed are those who throw a party!"

Humanist Service

Humanists embrace a secular view of life. Generally they do not believe in God but instead focus on man's joyful yet flawed (and brief) existence here on earth. The humanist funeral service is non-religious, but still seeks to acknowledge the life and death of the person who died. It also seeks to comfort survivors and help them support one another. As with all the other general service types, the humanist funeral service tends to include readings, music and memory-sharing—except that the readings and music emphasize life here on earth and do not imply there is life beyond the grave.

Committal Service

The committal (or commitment) service is held at the gravesite before the body or urn is buried, or in the chapel of a crematory prior to cremation. The committal is usually in addition to a funeral or memorial service and is the occasion at which those in attendance say their last goodbyes to the body. In cases of body burial, the committal service is usually held immediately following the funeral service. In cases when cremation follows the funeral service, the final committal may take place several days later at the cemetery, columbarium or scattering site. The committal service is often brief. However, if this is the only service to be held (in this case it is often referred to as graveside services), this service may be more lengthy and include additional elements of ceremony. For example, memories may be expressed (through a eulogy or less formal sharing of memories), music may be played, and readings such as poetry may be included. As an action of final goodbye, some people may want to place a flower or handful of dirt on the casket. Some family members may want to stay and assist in filling in the grave, while others may prefer not to. Children often find committal services helpful in that they are able to see where the body goes. Should your family make use of cremation, it can still be helpful to create some form of a committed ceremony around the cremated remains whether you bury them, place them in a niche in a columbarium, scatter them, or take them home (see page 26).

Home Funeral Service

While this idea is relatively new, it is gaining attention. People are starting to choose to have funerals for their loved ones within their homes, sometimes for economic or environmental reasons. It also provides a more hands-on, unique way to create a funeral. A home funeral guide can be hired to help coordinate the ceremony. While where you can bury a body is limited from state to state (a few do allow burial on private land), there are few restrictions to having a home ceremony. To learn more, visit Home Funeral Info (http://homefuneral.info), Home Funeral Directory (http://homefuneraldirectory.com), or Home Funeral Alliance (http://homefuneralalliance.org).

Notes on Service Type

_____

_____

Organ Donation

As a family you may be able to donate organs, tissues, and/or eyes to help others who are in need of life-saving or life-enhancing tranplants. "Solid organs" such as the heart, lung, kidneys, liver and pancreas can be donated by persons suffering from brain death. The person's body is kept on a machine called a ventilator even after the declaration of death to maintain blood flow to the organs and to allow families time to decide about organ donation. Should a person suffer a cardiac death (as opposed to brain death), the donation of tissues and eyes may still occur if the family wishes.

Following donation, the body of the person who died can be embalmed and/or cremated just as any other body would be. Viewing of the body is often still possible.

What Will Happen to the Body

Your family must choose not only the type of funeral service to hold, but also what will happen to the body and where it will be laid to rest.

Embalming

Embalming is how the funeral home temporarily preserves the body of the person who died so that the body can be viewed by the family. Embalming also allows a number of days to elapse before burial or cremation, thus giving family and friends time to prepare and gather for the funeral.

If the body is to be buried or cremated within a day or so of the death, embalming may not be necessary or required in most cases. However, since such speed is not always practical, embalming will allow your family the time you need to plan and carry out a meaningful ceremony.

"Viewing the body is a way of honoring the transition from life to death and saying our hellos on the pathway to our goodbyes."
— Alan Wolfelt

Obviously, should you choose to use a memorial service format with no body present, embalming may not be necessary. If possible, before you make that decision, please read the following information on why we often view the body.

Open or Closed Casket
Why do we often view the body?

Viewing the body is a way of honoring the transition from life to death and saying hellos on the pathway to our goodbyes.

When possible, I encourage families to spend some time with the body. You can do this publicly through a visitation or privately at the funeral home. If the death occurred at home or at the hospital, you may want to hold and say goodbye to the body there. Over and over again, families tell me that spending time with the body helped them come to terms with the death and begin to make the transition from life before the death to life after the death. Although it can be emotionally painful, time spent with the body is often helpful to many people.

The casket may be open for the visitation alone or for both the visitation and the funeral. For some, open casket visitations or funerals followed by cremation is an appropriate choice. In some cultures, however, viewing the body is considered inappropriate or is forbidden. We are well served to be very respectful of other people's decisions related to seeing and spending time with the body.

Even in cases where the body is not viewable (due to severe trauma, for example), I still encourage families to spend time in the presence of the closed casket. This helps them acknowledge the reality of the death and say goodbye in a more personal, real way.

However, spending time with the body is a very personal choice and my hope is that your family will honor each person's individual decisions in this matter. If you choose not to, for example, but others in your family would like to, try to find ways to accommodate everyone's needs. Be non-judgmental, compassionate, and caring about whatever a person decides about the body.

Cemetery Burial

Perhaps your family already owns a cemetery plot where this person will be buried. If not, maybe you've noticed a nice local cemetery. Your funeral director will know which cemeteries are nearby and would best meet your needs. He or she can help you purchase cemetery plots and set up ongoing landscaping care plans.

Entombment also takes place at a cemetery. It is placement of the casketed body in an above-ground structure called a mausoleum. When a casket is entombed, it is placed in an enclosure (called a crypt)and the front is usually sealed and faced with either marble or granite.

Many families choose burial or entombment at a nearby cemetery because it allows them to visit the gravesite as often as they would like. This helps them continue to feel close to the person who died, while still acknowledging they have died.

Cremation

Cremation is an increasingly popular means of handling a body after a death. However, many people don't know what happens during cremation. Perhaps the following explanation will help your family choose between cremation and body burial.

Cremation takes place at a building called a crematory or crematorium. Within the crematory is a special cremation chamber, or retort (pronounced REtort). The body is placed in a cremation container or casket and is slid into the cremation chamber. After the container or casket is placed in the cremation chamber, the chamber door is tightly sealed and the operator turns on the heat.

A gas jet creates a white hot heat in the back of the cremation chamber. Because of the intensity of the heat, the body ignites and burns until only bone fragments remain. This process takes approximately 2-3 hours.

After the cremation, the remains are collected in a metal tray. At this point the remains are small bone fragments. To further reduce them, the remains are placed in a processor and refined down to the consistency of coarse sand.

The white or grayish remains, often called cremated remains at this stage, are then sealed in a transparent plastic bag along with an identification tag. The bag weighs about 5 lbs. and is similar in size to a 5-lb. bag of sugar. Often the family requests that the cremated remains be placed in an urn, which can then be buried, placed in a niche in a columbarium, taken home or transported for scattering.

Cremation is a respectful, dignified process that feels right for many of today's families. However, some faiths prohibit or discourage cremation. If you plan to hold a religious funeral ceremony and/or have the remains buried in a church cemetery, be sure to ask whether or not cremation is permitted.

Remember, if you choose cremation, keep in mind that it does not limit your ability to spend time with the body or hold a meaningful ceremony. You may have a visitation period and a funeral service prior to the cremation. Or your family may spend time privately with the body before cremation followed by a public ceremony a day or two later with the urn present. I have observed that keeping the dead person's body present for the funeral ceremony often encourages more expressions of grief and authentic mourning. The body is the "ultimate death symbol" and makes the unreal ("How can they be dead?") become real.

Columbariums

Many cemeteries have an above-ground structure called a columbarium for permanent storage of cremated remains. Columbariums, which are constructed of durable materials such as bronze, marble, granite, brick, stone or concrete, offer an alternative to burial or scattering of cremated remains. You may purchase individual or family niches in a columbarium, much as you would purchase plots at a cemetery. Your funeral director can advise you on what is available in your area. Scattering gardens are becoming more and more popular as cremations have increased.

Combination of Service Choices and Disposition Choices

Allow me to summarize the various combinations available to you.

1. Direct Burial/Cremation

This is when there is no funeral service or memorial service, but instead simply final disposition of the body by the funeral home or memorial society. If you are considering direct burial or cremation, I plead with you to reconsider. Honoring the life and death of the person who died with some sort of ceremony—no matter how brief, how small or how informal— will help your family acknowledge the reality of the death and begin to heal. When no ceremony is held, it is as if the life and death of the person who died had no significance to anyone. Also, keep in mind that you may still hold a committal service at the graveside or crematory should you select direct burial.

2. ***Funeral, Affirmation, Humanist or Committal Service Followed By Burial, Entombment Or Cremation***
Funeral service followed by earth burial is still the most common combination in North America. However, cremation is becoming more and more popular and trends suggest that, in the future, cremation will become the most widely used form of final disposition.

3. ***Memorial Service Preceded Or Followed By Burial, Entombment or Cremation***
Because the body is not present at a memorial service, burial, cremation or entombment could take place before or after the service.

Regardless of the choices you make, think carefully about the many options available to you and your family. Slow down and plan. It is through planning that a meaningful experience of a funeral ceremony is born. And do remember that funeral directors, clergy, celebrants, and close friends who have done these things before can all be valuable resources to you. You are not alone!

Notes on What Will Happen to the Body

_____

_____

_____

Financial Considerations

Today the average funeral in the United States costs about $8,000. This includes the funeral home's services, casket and vault or grave liner, and miscellaneous costs such as flowers, obituaries, death certificates, honorariums, etc. According to the 2010 funeral price survey by the National Funeral Directors Association, the average funeral cost for an adult funeral is $7,775.00. This does not include cemetery fees (grave space, marker, and opening and closing the grave) which can run $1500 to $2500. You can spend much less than this or even more depending on the choices you make. Since each funeral is unique, the costs will vary.

What can your family afford to spend? Consider this before arriving at the funeral home for the arrangement conference. Remember to account for employee benefits, life insurance and other death benefits, cash contributions from friends and family and especially costs that may have been prepaid as you discuss your funeral budget. Planning a final tribute that is both affordable and meaningful is the goal here.

I believe that whatever you spend to create a personalized ceremony in honor of the person who died is money well spent. Keep in mind, however, that a meaningful funeral is not necessarily an expensive one. Those elements that make a funeral truly personalized—such as displaying photos of the person who died and offering opportunities for mourners to share memories—are often free. I often say that a meaningful funeral can include a full-piece orchestra and the Mormon Tabernacle Choir or a simple prayer and a song. Do what feels right for you and your family and don't let anyone pressure you to spend beyond your means.

Notes on Financial Considerations

_____

_____

_____

Planning The Meaningful Funeral Ceremony

The Elements of Funeral Ceremonies

You probably haven't planned many funerals before. You may not have attended many funerals before. So, let's remind ourselves of the different parts that make up most funeral services. Even among different faiths and cultures, funeral ceremonies throughout North America often include many of the same elements. Your faith or culture may have its own variations on these elements of ceremony.

When mere words are inadequate, many people find the ritual of ceremony helps them know what to do when they don't know what to do. Consider including some or all of these elements as you plan a funeral ceremony that will be meaningful to your family. Many families find that the more elements of ceremony they include, the more the funeral is likely to create that "sweet spot" of a meaningful experience. Through the years, I have discerned that it is through interfacing numerous elements of the funeral with the six needs of mourning (see p. 54) that we are able to create memorable funeral experiences.

The Visitation

Sometimes called the wake, calling hours, viewing, or review, the visitation is a time for friends and family to support one another in their grief. The body is often present in an open or unopened casket, allowing you and others who loved the person who has died to acknowledge the reality of the death and to have the privilege of saying goodbye.

"When public rituals fail, they fail because they were not inclusive in spirit."
— Robert Fulghum

Receiving friends through a visitation activates your support system and allows others to express their concern and love for you. They will remember you invited them and often stay more available to you in the months that follow the death. In other words, having a visitation encourages you to openly and honestly mourn the death.

Notes on the visitation

_____

_____

_____

_____

_____

The Service

The Eulogy

Also called the remembrance or the homily, the eulogy acknowledges the unique life of the person who died and affirms the significance of that life for all who shared in it.

The eulogy can be delivered by a clergy person, a family member or a friend of the person who died. Instead of a traditional eulogy delivered by one person, you may choose to ask several people to speak and share their memories. There is also a growing trend toward having people attending the funeral stand up and share a memory of the person who died. This works well, especially at smaller or less formal gatherings.

Who will lead the service?

This is a critical question that you will find addressed in detail on p. 19. Please keep in mind that the person you choose to lead the service will be pivotal in determining the tone and feel of the funeral. Do not appoint someone to lead the service without giving this issue sufficient thought.

If the person who will be delivering the eulogy didn't really know the person who died, make an effort to share with him or her anecdotes and memories that are important to you. Ask yourself, "What stands out to me about this person's life?" "What are some special memories I'd like to share?" "What were some times I felt particularly close to this person?" "What were some admirable qualities about this person?"

Often the eulogy is the most remembered and meaningful element of a funeral ceremony. Be creative as you discuss ways to share memories of the person who died. Try to avoid having someone who didn't really know the person who died give the eulogy. While some have learned to give excellent, personalized eulogies, other clergy members may speak a few generic words about the person who died or resort to sermonizing about life and death in lieu of personalizing their message. If your family would feel comforted by a religious sermon during the ceremony, by all means, ask a clergyperson to give one. Just be sure to have someone else (or several people) deliver a personalized eulogy in addition to the sermon.

The word eulogy comes from the Greek eulogia, meaning praise or blessing. This is the time to give thanks for a person's life and to honor his or her memory. This is not the time to bring up painful or difficult memories but to emphasize the good we can find in someone. You may privately mourn some of what you wished could have been different about this person, or your unique relationship with him or her; however, the public eulogy is not the time to do that!

Notes on the eulogy

_____

_____

_____

_____

_____

_____

_____

_____

Some tips for eulogy-givers

Writing and delivering a eulogy is a loving, important gesture that merits your time and attention over the next day or two. Though the task may seem daunting right now, you'll find that once you start jotting down ideas, your eulogy will come together naturally. Afterwards, many who attend the funeral will thank you for your contribution, and your eulogy will be cherished always by the family and friends of the person who died.

Here are some ideas to get you started.

- **Be brave.** The thought of writing a speech and presenting it in public makes many people anxious. Set aside your fears for now. You can do this. Focus on the person who died and the gift you will be giving to all who knew and loved him or her.

- **Think.** Before you start writing, go for a long walk or drive and think about the life of the person who died. This will help you collect your thoughts and focus on writing the eulogy.

- **Brainstorm.** Spend half an hour (longer if you want) writing down all the thoughts, ideas and memories that come to you.

- **Look at photos.** Flipping through photo albums may remind you of important qualities and memories of the person who died.

- **Don't try to do it all.** Your eulogy doesn't have to cover every aspect of this person's life. In fact, often the best eulogies are those that focus on the eulogy-giver's personal thoughts and memories. Do try to acknowledge those who were closest to the person who died as well as important achievements in the person's life, but don't feel obligated to create an exhaustive biography.

- **Ask others to share memories.** A good way to include others in the ceremony is to ask them to share thoughts and memories, which you can then incorporate into the eulogy.

- **Write a draft.** Once you've brainstormed and collected memories, it's time to write the first draft. Go somewhere quiet and write it all in one sitting, start to finish. Don't worry about getting it perfect for now—just get it down on paper.

- **Let it sit.** If time allows, let your eulogy draft sit for a few hours or a day before revising.

- **Get a second opinion.** Have someone else—preferably someone who was close to the person who died—read over your draft at this point. This person can make revision suggestions and help you avoid inadvertently saying something that might offend others.

- **Polish.** Read over your first draft. Look for awkward phrases or stiff wording. Improve the transitions from paragraph to paragraph or thought to thought. Find adjectives and verbs that really capture the essence of the person who died.

- **Present your eulogy with love.** Now you need to present your eulogy. You may well feel nervous, but if you can keep your focus on the person who died instead of your own fears, you'll loosen up. If you break down as you're talking, that's OK. Everyone will understand. Just stop for a few seconds, collect yourself and continue.

- **Speak up.** It's very important that you speak clearly and loudly so that everyone can hear you.

A Sample Eulogy

My editor, Karla Oceanak, recently wrote and delivered the eulogy at her grandmother's funeral. I hope this excerpt gives you some good ideas.

> *Mornings after I slept over at Nana's, I sat at her breakfast table and she fixed me oatmeal. All over the midwest, grandmothers were preparing oatmeal for their granddaughters, but hers was different, a suspiciously healthy kind she said was "steel-cut." To my relief it wasn't steely at all, but gooey hot and iced with melting brown sugar. With my silver Mickey Mouse spoon I skimmed the sugar while she flitted about the tiny galley kitchen.*
>
> *It is from this vantage point that I remember Nana best: me looking up at her in silent wonder, my silver-haired, brown-skinned fairy grandmother, while she raced from task to task, adventure to adventure. In her dining room, the western sun refracted through the facets of her cut crystal, showering the crimson wallpaper with tiny rainbows. Nana sparkled on me like that. Her admiring apprentice, I beheld her as she shimmered and shone. I think many of you probably regarded Gracie with the same awe and admiration. She was irrepressible. Exuberant. Vibrant. She loved life and she appreciated every moment. As my brother told me the other day, "Nana could light up a room."*

She certainly lit up my childhood. In fact, some of my earliest memories are of her and her house on the hill. I see her candying orange peel and making fudge in the kitchen, lighting candles for holiday meals in the dining room, opening stacks of mail from her many far-flung friends in her living room chair. Amy, Eric and I all remember well the Easter egg hunts at her house where, after church, she greeted us at her door with her dizzying welcome. "Oh, my dear ones, you beautiful children, come in, come in," as she hugged and kissed us quickly then rushed back to the kitchen, all the while gushing about her busy, lovely morning. Then we kids would be off with our Easter baskets, scouring the house from top to bottom for pastel foil-wrapped chocolate eggs.

Yes, Gracie was an optimist, even though she never led a life of privilege and ease. She worked hard. Her parents worked hard and expected the same of their children. At a young age, Gracie did household chores my kids couldn't comprehend. She helped earn money by selling smoked carp door to door. At 17 she taught country school.

Five years later Grace McGrew married Karl Anderson. She once told me the story of their courtship. An observant railroad worker seven years her senior, Karl decided that the quickest and most legitimate way to Gracie's heart was to abandon his Lutheran parish and begin attending Sunday services at Christ Church. This he did, bravely sitting by himself in the front pew. A few weeks later Karl requested a private conference with Father Barnett. That next Sunday, after Morning Prayer, Reverend Barnett called an oblivious young Gracie into his private quarters. "Karl Anderson is in love with you and will make you a good husband," he said. Six months later, they were married in the Old Frontenac Episcopal Church.

By all accounts, Gracie and Karl shared a beautiful 42 years together. They raised a son, Larry—my dad. They saved enough money to build their Cape Cod house on the hill. They gardened, hauling in 150 loads of topsoil so they could have a lawn and prize-winning flowerbeds atop the shale. While Karl worked as produce manager at Sundberg's, Gracie tended hearth and home, was active in the local horticultural society and served on the school board. They were also proud parents to their son, who excelled in high school sports and later served in the Navy.

Grace and Karl continued to attend and be active in Christ Church. Grace taught Sunday School and was the first vestrywoman. She volunteered for the state diocese. She loved this church and all its parishioners. I wonder how many church services she attended here in her 96 years?

After Karl died in 1967, the undaunted Gracie wheedled her way into becoming a hostess for Lund's new Penn Avenue grocery store. Get this: At Lund's, Gracie's job was to talk with customers, tell jokes, dispense advice about nutrition, and play penny ante poker with her boss over lunch. For this she was paid. For 23 years, Gracie gave herself to Lund's on Fridays and Saturdays, commuting to the Twin Cities even in the worst weather. And in return the people of Minneapolis gave themselves to Gracie. A Red Wing native with a lifelong love affair with this river town, Gracie made many, many friends in Minneapolis and became something of a celebrity. Many of you remember her stint as "Gracie the Grocery Shopper" on WCCO TV's "PM Magazine" during the late 70s.

And so we gather today to say goodbye to our Amazing Grace. I am so lucky, so grateful, to have had her as such a special part of my life. I know my father, mother, brother and sister feel the same. I'll bet many of you do, too, and I hope you'll share your own personal Gracie stories with us later.

We had Gracie with us a long time, didn't we? All that walking and tofu earned her some extra years, I'd say. But those of you who saw her recently knew that her quality of life was diminishing day by day. Her body was worn out. Her memory was fading fast. She'd been in a nursing home since late February—something she'd always dreaded. And even though she was in good spirits and making the staff laugh right up until the end, it was time. At 96, Gracie loved and outlived many friends and family. It's their turn to have her now. We'll all miss her, but it's time for her infectious, signature laugh to peal through the heavens.

When I asked Amy and Eric what they remembered most about Nana, they both mentioned the "one for the money" game. It's one of my favorite memories, too. I would stand at the first landing on the steps inside her entryway. Nana would stand at the bottom, four carpeted steps below. "One for the money," we'd giggle, "two for the show, three to get ready," me shouting now, "and four to go!" The afternoon sun backlit her joyful face, encircling her in a radiant halo. Her arms, always eager for our next embrace, stretched up and out to me. On cue I'd jump and she'd catch me, and our laughter would ricochet off the ceiling, the walls and out the open window to her beloved river valley below.

This vision of you glows in my past and lights my future, Nana. Again one day it will be my turn to make that great leap, and I will instinctively turn toward your radiance and jump with joy into your strong, waiting arms.

Music

Music is an important part of many social rituals. One of the purposes of music is to help us access our feelings, both happy and sad. During the funeral ceremony, music helps us think about our loss and embrace our painful feelings of grief. Consider music that was meaningful to the person who died or to your family. Most funeral homes and many churches and other places of worship have the capability to play CDs or music from iPods. Check out the quality of the sound system and if it doesn't meet your standards, find an outside source to provide a high quality system. If you'd like to have live singers or musicians, your funeral director or clergyperson can help you contact and schedule them. (Most funeral homes and churches have their own organists/pianists, for example.)

Notes on music

_____

_____

_____

_____

_____

_____

_____

_____

Memories

Memories are the most precious legacy we have after someone we love dies.

Your family can choose to provide opportunities for memory-sharing beyond the eulogy. As we all realize, not everyone feels comfortable speaking in front of a crowd. Some creative alternatives include:

- *Memory Baskets* - Provide a time and a place during the visitation or the funeral service where people can write down memories on paper and place them in a "memory basket." Some of these memories can be read during the eulogy or tacked on a board for others to read.

- *Memory Books* - Convert your registration book into a registration/memory book. Leave a column on the right-hand side of the registration book and encourage people not only to sign their names, but to write out a memory or two of the person who has died. Later, you can make copies of this book for everyone in the family. I can't recommend this enough!

- *Memory Tables or Memory Boards* - Many funeral homes make available tables or boards for families to display memorabilia and photos. If the person who died had a favorite hobby, consider setting up a display that represents this (e.g. model trains, photos of her garden, fishing tackle, etc.) Physical objects that link mourners to the person who died can be displayed, too (e.g. special articles of clothing, favorite toys for a child). You could also set out family photo albums and framed pictures. Memory tables give mourners a good place to gather and share memories of the person who died.

- *Memory DVDs* - Some funeral homes offer memory DVDs that incorporate visual images with music. There are a growing number of companies that can provide you with this service. Ask your funeral director for details.

- *Memory Letters* - Some friends and family members may want to write a personal letter to the person who died. These letters can then be sealed and placed in the casket or displayed near the casket for other mourners to read.

Through memories, those who have died live on in us. Be sure to talk to your funeral director about ways of sharing memories at this funeral.

Notes on ways to share memories

_____

_____

_____

_____

_____

_____

_____

_____

Recording the Service

Many funeral homes have the equipment to vidoetape and/or audiotape funeral ceremonies. More and more families are finding that capturing the funeral for posterity allows them to replay it later in their grief journeys, when they're not so overwhelmed and exhausted. The recording often becomes a cherished family keepsake. It can also be duplicated for friends and family who aren't able to attend the service.

Symbols

Symbols say for us what we could not possibly say in words at this time.

- Flowers
  Flowers represent love and beauty. Accepting flowers from friends is a way of accepting their support (respect cultural differences).

- Food
  Friends bring food as a way of nurturing mourners and demonstrating their support.

- Candles
  The flame of a candle represents the spirit. For some, it also represents life's continuation beyond death.

- The Body
  I often refer to the body of the person who died as the "ultimate symbol." Whether present in an open or unopened casket, the body serves as a focus for mourners and helps them acknowledge and embrace their pain. (It's like the American flag flying prominently when we gather to sing the National Anthem. Consider how disoriented and distracted the crowd would feel as they started to sing, "Oh say can you see..." and there was no flag in sight!) Sometimes when the body isn't present, those attending the funeral will say, "Wasn't that nice. Nobody even cried." Actually, a funeral without at least a few tears is a funeral at which people may be repressing their pain.

When words are inadequate, symbols and ritual help us express our thoughts and feelings.

Notes on symbols

_____

_____

_____

_____

_____

_____

_____

_____

_____

Including children in the funeral

Most of the rituals in our society focus on children. What would birthdays or Christmas be without kids? Unfortunately, the funeral ritual, whose purpose is to help mourners begin to heal, is often not seen as a ritual for kids. Too often, children are not included in the funeral because adults want to protect them. The funeral is painful, they reason, so I will shelter the children from this pain.

Yes, funerals can be very painful, but children have the same right and privilege to participate in them as adults do.

You can help appropriately include children by:

- Helping explain the funeral to children
  Unless they have attended one before, children don't know what to expect from a funeral. You can help by explaining what will happen before, during and after the ceremony. Give as many specifics as the child seems interested in hearing.

  If the body will be viewed either at a visitation or at the funeral itself, let the child know this in advance. Explain what the casket and the body will look like. If the body is to be cremated, explain what cremation means and what will happen to the cremated remains.

  You can also help children understand why we have funerals. Children need to know that the funeral is a time of sadness because someone has died, a time to honor the person who died, a time to help comfort and support each other and a time to affirm that life goes on.

- Finding age-appropriate ways for children to take part in the funeral
  When appropriate, you can encourage children to actually take part in the funeral. Grieving children feel included when they can share a favorite memory or read a special poem as part of the funeral. Shyer children can participate by lighting a candle or placing something special (a memento, a drawing, a letter or a photo, for example) in the casket. And many children feel more included when they are invited simply to help plan the funeral service.

- Understanding and accepting the child's way of mourning
  Understand that children often need to accept their grief in doses, and that outward signs of grief may come and go. It is not unusual, for example, for children to want to roughhouse with their cousins during the visitation or play video games right after the funeral. Respect the child's need to be a child during this extraordinarily difficult time.

The Procession

Also called the cortège, this is the funeral procession from the funeral service to the gravesite or columbarium, scattering garden, etc. It is usually led by the hearse containing the casketed body.

The procession is a symbol of mutual support and a public honoring of the death. Mourners accompany one another to the final resting place of the person who died. Often, even strangers take pause and are respectful because they know someone in your family has died.

Notes on the procession

_____

_____

_____

_____

_____

The Committal Service

The graveside service is the final opportunity to say goodbye. It is also a way of honoring the dead and helping them exit this life with honor, dignity and respect.

Accompanying a body to its final resting place and saying a few last words brings a necessary feeling of finality to the funeral process.

Even if you are having a full funeral service, I still encourage you to have a short committal service at the gravesite, mausoleum, columbarium or scattering site. The committal service gives a feeling of finality to the funeral that you'll never have otherwise.

Notes on the committal service

_____

_____

_____

_____

_____

_____

The Gathering or Reception

Most funerals are followed by a gathering of friends and family. This special and essential time allows your family and friends to tell stories about the person who died, to cry, to laugh, to support one another. It is an informal time of release after the more formal elements of the funeral ceremony. The gathering is also a transition, a rite of passage back to living again. It demonstrates the continuity of life, even in the face of death.

Some family members or friends may tell you that the gathering isn't necessary or that they'd prefer not to attend. It's OK if everyone can't (or chooses not to) be there. It's still a very important time for many of the people who will attend the service.

The reception can be held in your family home, in a park or in a church meeting room. Many funeral homes also have reception rooms. A buffet-style meal is usually served at the reception. Sometimes family and friends contribute food potluck-style and sometimes the meal is catered. Again, do what feels right for you and your family.

Notes on the gathering

_____

_____

_____

_____

_____

_____

_____

_____

Funeral Misconceptions

- Funerals make us too sad. When someone loved dies, we need to be sad. Funerals provide us with a safe place in which to embrace our pain.
- Funerals are inconvenient. Taking a few hours out of your week to demonstrate your love for the person who died and your support for survivors is not an inconvenience but a privilege.
- Funerals and cremation are mutually exclusive. A funeral (with or without the body present) may be held prior to cremation. Embalmed bodies are often cremated.

- Funerals require the body to be embalmed. Not necessarily. Depending on local health regulations, funerals held shortly after the death may require no special means of preservation.
- Funerals are only for religious people. Not true. Non-religious ceremonies are appropriate and very healing for some.
- Funerals are rote and meaningless. They needn't be. With forethought and planning, funerals can and should be personalized rituals reflecting the uniqueness of the bereaved family.
- Funerals should reflect what the dead person wanted. Maybe not . . . While the wishes of the person who died should be respected, funerals are primarily for the benefit of the living.
- Funerals are only for grown-ups. Anyone old enought to love is old enough to mourn. Children, too, should have the right and the privilege to attend funerals.

Ten Freedoms For Creating Meaningful Funeral Ceremonies

Meaningful funerals do not just happen. They are well-thought-out rituals that, at least for a day or two, demand your focus and your time. But the planning may feel less burdensome if you keep in mind that the energy you expend now to create a personalized, inclusive ceremony will help you, your family and other mourners embark on healthy, healing grief journeys.

The following list is intended to empower you to create a funeral that will be meaningful to you and your family and friends.

1. You have the freedom to make use of ritual.
2. You have the freedom to plan a funeral that will meet the unique needs of your family.
3. You have the freedom to ask friends and family members to be involved in the funeral.
4. You have the freedom to view the body before and during the funeral.
5. You have the freedom to embrace your pain during the funeral.
6. You have the freedom to plan a funeral that will reflect your spirituality.
7. You have the freedom to search for meaning before, during and after the funeral.
8. You have the freedom to make use of memory during the funeral.
9. You have the freedom to be tolerant of your physical and emotional limits.
10. You have the freedom to move toward your grief and heal.

Personalizing This Funeral Service

The funeral you are about to plan should be a meaningful, personalized tribute to the person who died. Think about his or her qualities and what he or she meant to others. Consider his or her passions, hobbies, pasttimes, likes, dislikes. How can you capture this unique life? Be creative as you, together with your family, friends, funeral director and the person who will lead the service, brainstorm how to remember and honor the person who died.

Attributes or passions of the person who died that we want to be sure to honor

_____
_____
_____
_____
_____
_____

Memories to share

_____
_____
_____
_____
_____
_____

Important people to include somehow

_____
_____
_____
_____
_____
_____
_____

Person to lead the ceremony_____

Others who might want to speak or share memories

_____

_____

_____

_____

_____

Honorary Roles at the Funeral
Consider including those who loved the person who died by asking them to be a part of the ceremony.
Pallbearears (usually 6)

_____

_____

_____

_____

_____

Honorary pallbearers _____

Ushers_____

Readers_____

Singer/musicians _____

Music ideas for the visitation_____

Music ideas for the ceremony

_____

_____

_____

_____

Readings ideas for the ceremony

_____

_____

_____

_____

_____

_____

_____

_____

_____

_____

Personal items we could display (at the visitation, the service and/or the gathering afterwards): Photos, collections, hobby paraphernalia, artwork and many other objects that tangibly depict the life of the person who died are meaningful and appropriate to display.

_____

_____

_____

_____

_____

_____

_____

_____

_____

_____

_____

_____

Some Ideas for Personalizing a Funeral Service

The funeral service you have should be as special as the life you will be remembering. Here are a few ideas:

• Write a personalized obituary. Some newspapers allow you to express a little more than the usual who/what/why/where/when. Appoint a creative "word" person in the family to handle this task.

• Create a column in the guest book for people to jot down a memory after they sign their name.

• Display personal items or hobby paraphernalia on a table at the visitation, the ceremony and/or the gathering afterwards.

• Have more than one person deliver the eulogy. Ask several people to share memories and talk about different aspects of the person who died.

• Choose clothing for the person who died that reflects his or her life, interests, passions, etc. The clothing needn't be formal or somber!

• Create a personalized program for the ceremony. You can include photos, poems, anecdotes—whatever you'd like! Your funeral director can help you with this.

• Show a DVD or slide show of the person's life during the funeral. Pictures tell a thousand words!

• Ask children if they would like to write a letter or draw a picture for the person who died. Their "goodbyes" can then be placed in the casket alongside the body.

• Select flowers that were meaningful to the person who died. A simple arrangement of freshly-cut lilacs, for example, might be perfect.

• At the funeral, invite people to write down a memory of the person who died. Appoint someone to gather and read the memories aloud.

• Create a funeral that captures the personality of the person who died. If he was zany, don't be afraid to use humor. If she was affectionate, have everyone stand up and hug the person next to them during the ceremony.

• Display photos of the person who died at the visitation, the ceremony and/or the gathering. In fact, putting together a photo collage can be a very healing experience for the family in the days before the funeral.

• Use lots of music, especially if music was meaningful to the person who died or is to your family. Music can be played at the visitation, the committal service and the gathering as well as the funeral service itself!

• Create a personalized grave marker. Include a poem, a drawing or a short phrase that defines the person who died.

Glossary Of Funeral Terms

Arrangement conference - The meeting with the funeral director in which you will discuss your wishes for the funeral and the disposition of the body.

Burial - Also called interment, earth burial at a cemetery is the most traditional and still the most common method for final disposition of the body.

Celebrant - A person who provides personalized services to a family to create a meaningful ceremony or ritual during a life transition.

Columbarium - An above-ground structure for final disposition of cremated remains. Many cemeteries have a columbarium where individual or family niches may be purchased.

Committal service - This is the brief graveside ceremony held with the casket or urn present before it is lowered into the ground.

Cremation - Cremation involves reducing the body through intense heat to cremated remains. After cremation, the remains can be buried, entombed, scattered or retained by the family.

Crypt - An above-ground burial site in a mausoleum.

Direct cremation - Cremation without a funeral. Direct cremation bypasses the healing process of planning and taking part in a personalized funeral ceremony.

Embalming - Embalming preserves the body for a number of days following the death, allowing for the family to view the body and hold the funeral service on a day that is convenient for out-of-town friends and relatives. Embalming is not, however, mandatory.

Entombment - Placement of the casket in an above-ground structure called a mausoleum.

Funeral - The ceremony that honors the end of a person's life.

Grave Liner - Similar to a vault in purpose and construction, grave liners are usually simpler and less expensive.

Honorarium - The fee typically paid to a clergyperson or celebrant for officiating the funeral ceremony and to musicians or soloists for their contributions.

Mausoleum - A small building in a cemetery, a mausoleum is like a burial plot above ground. When a casket is entombed, it is placed in an enclosure (called a crypt) and the front is usually sealed and faced with stone.

Niche - One of a number of recesses in the wall of a columbarium. The niche may be open-front, protected by glass (this option allows viewing of the urn), or closed-front, faced with bronze, marble or granite. The urn containing the cremated remains is placed inside the niche and the front is sealed.

Obituary - A notice in the newspaper that announces the death to the community, summarizes the person's life and invites readers to attend the funeral and/ or make memorial contributions in the name of the person who died. Usually the funeral director will handle submitting the pertinent information to the newspaper and newspaper staff will write the obituary. Some newspapers, however, will allow you to write your own more personalized obituary. Most newspapers do not charge a fee for obituaries, but be aware that some do. As newspapers have lost revenue, they are now beginning to charge for this service.

Pallbearers - The people who carry the casket from the ceremony to the hearse and from the hearse to the gravesite. Usually there are six pallbearers and they are traditionally male. If there are more friends than are needed (or friends who are unable to carry the heavy casket), make them honorary pallbearers.

Urn - A small vase-like container specially designed for holding cremated remains.

Vault - A concrete or metal container into which the casket is placed before burial at a cemetery. Today, vaults are required by most cemeteries because they stabilize the grave site, preventing the earth from settling above the casket.

Visitation - Visitation is a scheduled time for family and friends to see the person who died, perhaps for the final time. Viewing the body often helps families acknowledge the reality of the death and grants them the privilege of saying hello on the pathway to goodbye.

Afterwords...
Understanding Grief

"The act of living is different all through. Her absence is like the sky, spread all over everything."
— C.S. Lewis, A Grief Observed

Someone you love has died. You are beginning a journey that is often frightening, painful and sometimes lonely. No words, written or spoken, can take away the pain you now feel. I hope, however, that this information will bring you some comfort and encouragement as you make a commitment to help yourself heal.

Perhaps someone has already said to you, "In time, you'll feel better." Actually, time alone has nothing to do with healing. To heal, you must be willing to learn about and understand the grief process and how it will affect you today, tomorrow and forever. Grief waits on a welcome, not on time.

As scary as this may sound, you will never "get over" your grief. Instead, you will learn to live with it. This does not mean that you will never be happy again. On the contrary, many bereaved people who have moved toward healing find their lives even fuller and more meaningful than they were before the death of someone loved. If you allow yourself the time and compassion to mourn, if you truly work through your grief, you too will heal. You too will go on to find continued meaning in living and loving.

What you may feel

So what can you expect in the weeks and months ahead? It depends. You see, grief is different for every person. It may also feel different for you now than it did if someone close to you died in years past. Grief is never the same twice.

While your grief is unique, it might help you to understand some of the most common emotions associated with grief:

• **Shock.** You may feel dazed and stunned, especially during the time immediately following the death. This feeling is nature's way of protecting you from an overwhelming reality. You may experience heart palpitations, queasiness, stomach pains or dizziness. You may also find yourself crying hysterically, screaming angrily or even laughing. These behaviors help you survive during this extraordinarily difficult time.

- **Confusion**. After the death of someone loved, you may feel a sense of ongoing confusion. It's like being in the middle of a wild, rushing river where you can't get ahold of anything. Disconnected thoughts race through your mind and you may be unable to complete tasks. As part of your confusion, you might also experience a sense of the dead person's presence or even have fleeting glimpses of the person across the room. I call this latter experience, which is very common and very normal, a "memory picture."

- **Anxiety**. As your head and heart begin to miss the person who died, you may naturally feel anxious. You may fear that you or others you love will die, too. You may doubt your ability to survive without the person who died. You may feel anxious about everyday realities, such as work or finances. You may even panic as you think through the repercussions of this death.

- **Anger**. Anger and its cousins hate, blame, terror, resentment, rage and jealousy are normal responses to the death of someone loved. With loss comes the desire to protest. Explosive emotions such as these provide the vehicle to do so. If feelings like these are part of your grief journey, be aware that you have two avenues for expressing them: outward or inward. The outward avenue leads to healing; the inward avenue does not. Critical to your healing is finding someone who doesn't judge you but allows you to feel whatever you feel.

- **Guilt**. When someone you care about dies, it's natural to consider the "if-only's": If only I had died instead. If only I had told her to buckle her seatbelt. You may also feel guilty if a part of you feels relief—common after extended illnesses or as a product of ambivalent relationships. While these feelings of guilt or regret are natural, they are sometimes not logical to those around you. But remember—thinking is logical; feeling is not.

- **Sadness**. Someone you love has died, and you hurt. Your full sense of loss will not occur all at once. Weeks or often months will pass before you are fully confronted with the depths of your sadness. This slow progression is good. You could not and should not tolerate all of your sadness at once. Your body, mind and spirit need time working together to allow you to embrace the depth of your loss. Be patient with yourself.

You may also experience physiological changes as part of your grief. Actually, one literal definition of the word "grievous" is causing physical suffering. You may be shocked by how much your body responds to the impact of your loss. Among the most common physical responses to loss are trouble with sleeping and low energy. You may have trouble getting to sleep or you may wake up early in the morning and have trouble getting back to sleep. You may also find yourself feeling more tired than usual.

Muscle aches and pains, shortness of breath, feelings of emptiness in your stomach, tightness in your throat or chest, digestive problems, sensitivity to noise, nausea, headaches, increased allergic reactions, changes in appetite, weight loss or gain, agitation and generalized tension—all are ways your body may react to the loss of someone loved.

Good self-care is important at this time. The stress of grief can suppress your immune system and make you more likely to experience physical problems. See a physician for specific physical symptoms that concern you.

Myths about grief

If you are to heal, you must first become aware of and dispel a few common myths about grief and mourning. Don't condemn yourself or others if, as you read this section, you realize you believe in some of these myths. Instead, make use of any new insights to help you accomplish your work of mourning in a healthier way.

- **Myth #1: There are predictable stages to grief.**
  You have probably already heard about the "stages of grief." Somehow the notion of stages comforts people as they try to make sense of death. "If only I can get through these first two stages," they might think to themselves, "I'll be O.K." While grief often manifests itself in similar ways, and at times there is a logical progression of emotion, grief is not predictable. It is tempestuous and fickle, revisiting its earlier emotions without warning, bounding here and there, sometimes skipping "stages" altogether. Let your own personal experience with grief guide you. Often, it is more helpful to think of "dimensions" of grief than it is to think of "stages" of grief.

- **Myth #2: We should avoid the painful parts of grieving.**
  Our society often encourages prematurely moving away from grief instead of toward it. The result is too many bereaved people either grieving in isolation or running away from their grief. Far too many people view grief as something to be overcome rather than experienced. When you avoid the pain of grief, you avoid healing. Instead, you must learn to slowly embrace the full force of this pain so that someday you can again embrace happiness.

- **Myth #3: We should "get over" our grief as soon as possible.**
  Instead of the traditional term used to describe the final "stage" of grief—resolution or recovery—I prefer the word reconciliation. Reconciliation does not mean getting over your grief, it means growing through it. Reconciliation has no preset timetable and can be unique to the many influences of your grief. However, as you allow yourself to mourn you will feel a renewed sense of energy and confidence, an ability to fully acknowledge the reality of the death, and the capacity to become reinvolved with the activities of living. You will also come to acknowledge that pain and grief are difficult but necessary parts of living.

Helping Yourself Heal

I have had the privilege to work with thousands of bereaved people. I have also experienced a number of significant losses in my own life. From these grief journeys I have learned one critical lesson: those who grieve without mourning do not integrate loss into their lives.

Mourning in our culture isn't always easy. Most people try to avoid pain and other feelings of loss. Why? Because the role of suffering is misunderstood. Normal thoughts and feelings connected to loss are typically seen as unnecessary and sometimes shameful. Society wrongly implies that if you, as a bereaved person, openly express your feelings of grief, you are immature. If your feelings are fairly intense, you may be labeled "overly emotional" or even "crazy." Instead of encouraging you to express yourself, our culture's unstated rules would have you avoid your hurt and "be strong."

If you take these grief-repressive messages to heart, you may become powerless to help yourself heal. To think that mourning is wrong may tempt you to act as if you feel better than you really do. Ultimately, if you deny your emotions, you deny the essence of life.

To integrate loss into your life, you must also acknowledge that you are not a "patient" who needs someone to do something to make you feel better. Grief is not a disease. Instead, it is the normal, healthy process of coping with the death of someone loved. And while no "treatment" exists for what you are feeling, I promise you that if you can see yourself as an active participant in your healing, you will experience a renewed sense of meaning and purpose in your life.

The Six Reconciliation Needs of Mourning

While your grief journey will be unique, all mourners have certain needs that must be met if they are to heal. I call six of the most central of these "The Reconciliation Needs of Mourning." Though these needs are numbered one through six, do not interpret them as orderly steps on the road to healing. Instead, you will probably find yourself bouncing back and forth from one to the other, and maybe even working on two or more simultaneously.

Reconciliation vs. Resolution

In many grief models, the final "stage" of grief is referred to as resolution. You may also hear the term recovery. The problem with these definitions is that people do not "get over" grief; mourners are forever changed by the experience.

Reconciliation is a term I find more appropriate for what occurs as the mourner works to integrate the new reality of moving forward in life without the physical presence of the person who has died. With reconciliation comes a renewed sense of energy and confidence, an ability to fully acknowledge the reality of the death, and a capacity to become reinvolved in the activities of living. There is also an acknowledgment that pain and grief are difficult yet necessary parts of life.

Need 1. Acknowledge the reality of the death.
Whether the death was sudden or anticipated, acknowledging the full reality of the loss may take weeks, months, or sometimes years. You may move back and forth between protesting and encountering the reality of the death. You may discover yourself replaying events surround the death and confronting memories, both good and bad. It's as if each time you talk it out, the event is a little more real.

Need 2. Move toward the pain of the loss.
Expressing your thoughts and feelings about the death with all of their intensity is a difficult but important need. You will probably discover that you need to "dose" yourself when experiencing your pain. In other words, you cannot nor should not try to meet this need all at once.

Need 3. Continue the relationship with the person who died through memory.
Embracing your memories—both happy and sad—can be a very slow and, at times, painful process that occurs in small steps. But remembering the past makes hoping for the future possible.

Need 4. Develop a new self-identity.
Part of your self-identity comes from the relationships you have created with other people. When someone with whom you have a relationship dies, your self-identity naturally changes. Many people discover that as they move forward in their grief journeys, they find that some aspects of their self-identities have been positively changed. You may feel more confident, for example, or more open to life's challenges.

Need 5. Search for meaning.
When someone loved dies, you naturally question the meaning and purpose of

life. Coming to terms with those questions is another need you must meet if you are to progress in your grief journey. Move at your own pace as you recognize that allowing yourself to hurt and find ongoing meaning in your life will blend into each other, with the former overtaking the latter as healing occurs.

Need 6. Continue to receive support from others.
You will never stop needing the love and support of others because you never "get over" your grief. As you learn to reconcile your grief, however, you will need help less intensely and less often. So, while you probably won't need to see a counselor forever, you will always need your friends and family members to listen and support you in your continuing grief journey. Support groups can be another long-term helping resource.

Reaching out for help

When someone you love dies, you must mourn if you are to heal. But healing also requires the support and understanding of those around you as you embrace the pain of your loss.

Perhaps the most compassionate thing you can do for yourself at this difficult time is to reach out for help from others. Think of it this way: grieving may be the hardest work you have ever done. And hard work is less burdensome when others lend a hand. Life's greatest challenges—getting through school, raising children, pursuing a career—are in many ways team efforts. So it should be with mourning.

Friends and family members can often form the core of your support system. Seek out people who encourage you to be yourself and who acknowledge your many thoughts and feelings about the death. What you need most now are car-ing, non-judgmental listeners.

You may also find comfort in talking to a clergyperson. When someone loved dies, it is natural for you to feel ambivalent about your faith and question the very meaning of life. A clergy member who responds not with criticism but with empathy to all your feelings can be a valuable resource.

A professional counselor may also be a very helpful addition to your support system. In fact, a good counselor can be something friends and family members can't: an objective listener. A counselor's office can be that safe haven where you can "let go" of those feelings you're afraid to express elsewhere. What's more, a good counselor will then help you constructively channel those emotions.

For many grieving people, support groups are one of the best helping resources. In a group, you can connect with others who have experienced similar thoughts and feelings. You will be allowed and gently encouraged to talk about the person who died as much and as often as you like.

Your funeral home may sponsor a grief support group or have a list of grief resources in your community. Call your funeral director and ask.

Remember, help comes in different forms for different people. The trick is to find the combination that works best for you and then make use of it.

The truth about grief is that it requires the support and compassion of those around us. It is humbling and bigger than us. As you allow yourself to surrender to your need to authentically mourn, please keep in mind that mourning by definition is "the shared social response" to loss. We are well-served to not try to walk this walk alone and in isolation. Find some compassionate people to companion you and bear witness to your need to openly and honestly mourn.

Ongoing Ways Of Honoring
And Remembering The Life

Thank goodness for memory. It allows us to continue to embrace our love for the person who died. And remembering helps us integrate loss into our lives. Each time we conjure up a memory, we are finding a way both to acknowledge the reality of the death AND, most importantly, stoke the fires of our love for that person.

Soon after the death you will probably find yourself replaying memories of the person who died over and over again. This is normal and necessary. Allow yourself the time and space you need to remember. It is also important to share your memories with others. Talking about them will help you reconcile your loss.

In the months and years to come, more formal ways of remembering the person who died and honoring the life that was lived will help you and other mourners continue to heal and live life to its fullest. Here are some ideas.

Honor Special Days

Certain days, such as the anniversary of the death, the birthday of the person who died, holidays and other meaningful dates in your family, will probably be difficult for you. A good way to embrace your grief on these days is to make a point of honoring the person who died. Maybe you and other family members could plan to:

• Gather for a prayer or short service at the gravesite, mausoleum or location of scattering.

• Have prayers said or altar flowers placed at your church.

• Place a memorial ad in the newspaper.

• As a family, do something that the person who died liked to do.

• Prepare and share a favorite meal of the person who died.

• Gather in a circle and, one by one, share a memory of the person who died.

On these special days, DON'T avoid talking about or remembering the person who died. Repressing your normal thoughts and feelings will only make you feel worse. Instead, actively remember the person who died through shared activities and memory-swapping.

Record Your Memories

In this the age of technology and information, there are many means of recording memories at your disposal. Here are just a few:

- Pack a memory box. Include photos, newspaper clippings, small objects that belonged to the person who died, etc.

- Make a memory book. Similar to a memory box but in scrapbook form. Scrapbooking is a very popular hobby today and most discount and stationery stores carry wonderful materials.

- Put together a memory DVD. Do you have videotaped footage of the person who died? Watching the person you loved move and smile and hearing that special voice can be very healing. But finding those bits and pieces of footage in what may be stacks and stacks of videotapes isn't very convenient. Appoint the video/computerphile in your family to edit footage all onto one DVD, set it to music, etc.

- Create a Web page. Many people have created personalized Web pages in memory of loved ones. Maybe your family would like to design a cyber-memorial, too, complete with photos, video footage, text and music.

- Keep a journal. Even if you don't think of yourself as a writer, consider keeping a journal in the months ahead. It doesn't have to be fancy. Just get a notepad or loose-leaf binder and go to it. You don't have to share it with anyone unless you want to.

- Write a poem or a song or a letter. Writing a poem, a song or a letter is a great, unique way to remember someone who has died. Maybe you could share it with someone you know will understand and support your expression of precious memories.

- Make lists. List all of the things you want to remember about the person who died. List the things you found of value in the service you had. List the people you feel safe talking to about your grief.

Create a Memorial

Ongoing tributes to the person who died can give your grief a positive outlet. Get together with family and friends and brainstorm fitting ideas to honor the person you all loved so much. A couple ideas to get you jumpstarted:

- Start a foundation. Perhaps your family could start a charitable foundation in the name of the person who died. What did he or she believe strongly in? Your foundation could give an annual scholarship or support an important cause— whatever helps carry on the life of the person who died. Your accountant can help you with the details.

- Plant a tree. Public parks and open spaces are good candidates for memorial trees, benches, fountains, flower gardens, etc. Work with your city to find an appropriate place and time, then have friends and family gather for a short ceremony to dedicate the memorial. This type of memorial also gives mourners a place to visit when they want to embrace their grief and remember the person who died.

Have a Ceremony

Ritual and ceremony can help your family heal long after the funeral. Consider creative ways to use readings, memory-sharing, music and symbols to honor the life of the person who died and help your family heal.

- Have another memorial service. On the anniversary of the death, hold a less formal memorial service at your place of worship or home. Follow the short ceremony with a meal and socializing.

- Have a candle-lighting ceremony. In this memory-sharing activity, mourners gather around a table, each holding a small candle. A larger candle is lit in the center of the table and mourners take turns sharing memories and lighting their candles from the center candle. At the end, a prayer is said or music is played in memory of the person who died.

- Participate in a hospice ceremony. Many hospices have annual ceremonies in honor of clients who have died. If the person in your life who died was a hospice client, check with the bereavement coordinator for ongoing opportunities to gather for prayer and memory-sharing.

A Final Word

I hope you find comfort and guidance in this resource. I truly believe that while a funeral cannot change what has happened—the death of someone precious to you—it can and will make a significant difference in how you channel your grief toward healing. Even though I was trained as a "talk therapist" through twelve years of higher education, I discovered that families in grief are truly helped by ceremony. When words are inadequate, the ritual of ceremony is both fitting and healing.

I have often found that people who take the time and effort to create meaningful funeral arrangements when someone loved dies end up making new arrangements in their own lives. As time allows, drop me a note and let me know how your unique ceremony helped meet your needs and the needs of your family and friends.

Thank you for taking the time to read this and to reflect on the importance of creating a meaningful funeral not only in honor of the person who has died, but in honor of the needs of those who still live.

Recommended Readings

Acterberg, Jeanne, *Rituals of Healing*, New York: Bantam Books, 1989.

Ardinger, Barbara, A Woman's Book of Rituals and Celebrations, New York: New World Library, 1995.

Baum, Rachel R., *Funeral and Memorial Service Readings, Poems and Tributes*, McFarland Press: Jefferson, NC , 2007.

Brener, Anne, Mourning & Mitzvah, *A Guided Journal for Walking the Mourner's Path Through Grief to Healing*, Vermont: Jewish Lights Publishing, 1993.

Cahill, Sedonia, *The Ceremonial Circle: Practice, Ritual and Renewal*, San Francisco: Harper Collins, 1992.

Childs-Growell, Elaine, *Good Grief Rituals: Tools for Healing*, Station Hill Press, 1992.

Cole, D., *After Great Pain: A New Life Emerges*, New York: Summit Books, 1992.

Doka, Kenneth, *Disenfranchised Grief*, Lexington, Massachusetts: Lexington Books, 1989.

Donnelly, Katherine Fair, *Recovering from the Loss of a Sibling*, New York: Dodd, Mead and Co., 1988.

Driver, Tom Faw, *The Magic of Ritual: Our Need for Liberating Rites that Transform*, San Francisco: Harper Collins, 1991.

Feinstein, David, *Personal Mythology: The Psychology of Your Evolving Self*, New York: Tarcher, Inc., 1988.

Fulghum, Robert, *From Beginning to End: The Rituals of Our Lives*, New York: Villard Books, 1995.

Gillis, John, *A World of Their Own Making: Myth, Ritual and the Quest*, Boston: Basic Books, 1996.

Glass-Koentop, Pattalee, *Year of Moons, Season of Threes*, Boston: Llewellyn Publications, 1991.

Gootman, Marilyn, *When a Friend Dies*, Minneapolis: Free Spirit, 1994.

Hammerschlag, Carl A., *The Thief of the Spirit: Journey to Spiritual Healing*, New York: Simon and Schuster, 1993.

Harris, Jill W., *Remembrances and Celebrations: A Book of Eulogies*, Elegies, Letters and Epitaphs, New York: Pantheon Books, 1999.

Harrison, Jane, *Ancient Art and Ritual*, New York: H. Holt and Co., 1913.

Heffernan, William, *Ritual*, New York: New American Library, 1988.

Hirschfield, Jane, *Women in Praise of the Sacred*, New York: Harper Collins, 1994.

Imber-Black, Evan, *Rituals for Our Times: Celebrating, Healing and Changing Our Lives*, New York: Harper Collins, 1992.

James, Edwin, *Christian Myth and Ritual: A Historical Study*, Meridian Books, 1965.

Metrick, S.B., *Crossing the Bridge: Creating Ceremonies for Grieving and Healing from Life's Losses*, Berkeley: Celestial Arts, 1994.

Moffat, Mary Jane, *In the Midst of Winter—Selections from the Literature of Mourning*, New York: Vantage Press, 1982.

Morgan, John, *Young People and Death*, Philadelphia: Charles Press, 1991.

Morgenson, G., *Greeting the Angels: An Imaginal View of the Mourning Process*, Amityville, New York: Baywood Publishing Co., 1995.

Munro, Eleanor C., *Readings for Remembrance*, New York: Penguin USA, 2000.

Nelson, Gertrud, *To Dance with God: Family Ritual and Community Celebration*, Paulist Press, 1986.

Noel, Brook and Pamela Blair, PhD. *I Wasn't Ready to Say Goodbye: Surviving, Coping and Healing After the Sudden Death of a Loved One*, Milwaukee: Champion Press, 2008.

Paladin, Lynda S., *Ceremonies for Change: Creating Personal Ritual to Heal Life's Hurts*, Walpole, New Hampshire: Stillpoint Publishing International, 1991.

Roberts, Janice and Joy Johnson, *Thank You for Coming to Say Goodbye*, Omaha: Centering Corp., 1994.

Rushton, Lucy, *Death Customs*, Cincinnati: Thomason Learning, 1993.

Scruggs, Anderson, *Ritual for Myself*, New York: Macmillan Publishing, 1941.

Silverman, Morris, *Prayers of Consolation*, New York: Prayer Book Press, 1953.

Some, Malidoma, *Ritual: Power, Healing and Community*, Swan/Raven Press, 1993.

Stein, Diane, *Casting the Circle: A Woman's Book of Rituals*, Crossing Press, 1990.

Strocchia, Sharon, *Death Ritual in Late Imperial and Modern China*, Los Angeles: University of California, 1988.

Watts, Alan, *Myth and Ritual in Christianity*, New York: Vanguard Press, 1953.

Webb, Nancy Boyd, *Helping Bereaved Children*, New York: Guilford Press, 1993.

Williamson, Gay and David, *Transformative Rituals: Celebrations for Personal Growth*, Deerfield Beach, Florida: Health Communications, Inc., 1994.

Wolfelt, Alan, *Creating Meaningful Funeral Ceremonies: A Guide for Caregivers*, Fort Collins, Colorado: Companion Press, 1994.

Wolfelt, Alan, *Death and Grief: A Guide for Clergy*, Fort Collins, Colorado: Accelerated Development Inc, 1988.

Wolfelt, Alan, *The Journey Through Grief: Reflections on Healing*, Fort Collins, Colorado: Companion Press, 1996.

Wolfelt, Alan, Understanding Your Grief: Ten Essential Touchstones for Finding Hope and Healing Your Heart, Companion Press: Fort Collins, Colorado, 2003.

York, Sarah, *Remembering Well: Rituals for Celebrating Life and Mourning Death*, Jossey Bass: San Francisco, 2000.

Zunin, Lenard and Hilary, *The Art of Condolence*, New York: Harper Collins, 1991.

Organizations For Mourners

The following organizations are potential sources of information, education and referral.

Funerals and Related Matters: National Organizations

International Cemetery, Cremation & Funeral Association
107 Carpenter Drive, Suite 100
Sterling, VA 20164
Telephone: 703.391.8400
Toll-Free: 800.645.7700
Fax: 703.391.8416
Web site: http://www.iccfa.com

Cremation Association of North America
401 N. Michigan Avenue
Chicago, IL 60611
312-245-1077
E-mail: info@cremationassociation.org

International Order of the Golden Rule
3520 Executive Center Drive, Suite 300
Austin, TX 78731
512-334-5504 or 800-637-8030
E-mail: info@ogr.org

National Funeral Directors Association
13625 Bishop's Drive
Brookfield, WI 53005
1-800-228-6332
Web site: http://www.nfda.org
E-mail: nfda@nfda.org

Selected Independent Funeral Homes
500 Lake Cook Road, Suite 205
Deerfield, IL 60015
1-800-323-4219
Web site: http://www.selectedfuneral-homes.org

National Self-Help Organizations and Support Groups

AARP, Widowed Persons Services
Independent branches of this organization can be found by searching online for Widowed Persons Service and the name of your town or state.
Web site: http://www.aarp.org
information and resources; referrals to support groups

American Association of Suicidology
5221 Wisconsin Avenue, NW
Washington, DC 20015
202-237-2280
1-800-273-TALK (Suicide prevention lifeline)
Web site: http://www.suicidology.org
information and resources; referrals to suicide survivor groups

Center for Loss and Life Transition
3735 Broken Bow Road
Fort Collins, CO 80526
970-226-6050
Web site: http://www.centerforloss.com
E-mail: DrWolfelt@centerforloss.com
resources, education, training and referral for bereaved families; provides a certificate program in Death and Grief studies for bereavement professionals

The Compassionate Friends
900 Jorie Blvd., Suite 78
Oak Brook, IL 60523
877-969-0010
Web site:
http://www.compassionatefriends.org
information and resources for bereaved families who have experienced the death of a child

The Dougy Center
P.O. Box 86852
Portland, OR 97286
503-775-5683
Web site: http://www.dougy.org
E-mail: help@dougy.org
information, education, referral and support for children and families; publishes
a national directory on support programs
for bereaved children

Share
401 Jackson Street
St. Charles, MO 63301
1-800-821-6819
Web site: http://www.nationalshare.org
pregnancy and infant loss support

Mothers Against Drunk Driving (MADD)
511 E. John Carpenter Freeway, Ste
700,
Irving, TX 75062-8187
214-744-6233; 800-GET-MADD
Web site: http://www.MADD.org
education, resources and advocacy for
bereaved families

Parents of Murdered Children, Inc.
100 E. 8th Street, Suite 200
Cincinnati, OH 45202
513-721-5683; 888-818-POMC
Web site: http://www.pomc.com
E-mail: NatlPOMC@aol.com
information, resources and support for
bereaved families

National Hospice and Palliative Care
Organization - NHPCO
1731 King Street, Suite 100
Alexandria, VA 22314
1-800-658-8898
Web site: http://www.nhpco.org

National Institute of Mental Health Public
Inquiries
NIH Neuroscience Center
6001 Executive Blvd., Rm
8184 MSC 9663
Bethesda, MD 20892
Web site: http://www.nimh.nih.gov
E-mail: nimhinfo@nih.gov
education and publications for families
and professionals

Funeral Planning Summary Worksheet

Use this worksheet to help you summarize your thoughts and decisions about the funeral you are planning. Once completed, this worksheet can be photocopied for distribution to other friends and family members who may need detailed information in order to help with the ceremony.

Where appropriate, I have referred you to relevant text in other sections of this book so that you can refer back for more information.

Name of the person who died

_____

Date of birth_____ Date of death_____

Funeral home (See p. 13.)_____

Funeral director_____

Address_____

Phone number(s)_____

What Will We Do With The Body? (See p. 25.)

Checkboxes:

Body burial   Cremation

Cemetery_____

Scattering location or placement of cremated remains:

_____

Phone Numbers: _____

The Visitation (See p. 31.)

Date(s)_____   Time_____

Location_____

Address_____

Memory displays

_____

_____

_____

_____

Other details

_____

_____

_____

The Funeral Service

Date_____   Time_____

Location_____

Address_____

Checkboxes: Open casket _____ Closed casket_____ (See p. 25.)

Person to lead the ceremony (See p. 19.)

Name_____

Phone number(s)_____

Person (or people) to give the eulogy (See p. 32.)

Name_____

Phone number_____

Name_____

Phone number_____

Readers

Name_____ Phone_____

Reading_____

Name_____ Phone_____

Reading_____

Name_____ Phone_____

Reading_____

Name_____ Phone_____

Reading_____

Music (See p. 37.)

Selection_____

Played/sung by_____

Selection_____

Played/sung by_____

Selection_____

Played/sung by_____

Selection_____

Played/sung by_____

Pallbearears (usually 6)

Name_____ Phone_____

Name_____ Phone_____

Name_____ Phone_____

Name_____ Phone_____

Name_____ Phone_____

Name_____ Phone_____

Honorary pallbearers

Name_____ Phone_____

Name_____ Phone_____

Ushers (if different than pallbearers)

Name_____ Phone_____

Name_____ Phone_____

Name_____ Phone_____

Name_____ Phone_____

Memory Table, Box, Book, Board, etc. (See p. 37.)

What_____

Who's in charge_____
Phone_____

Things to include_____

_____

_____

(Checkbox) Will this service be recorded? Audiotape   Videtape

Who's in charge_____

Phone_____

Procession (See p. 41.)

Details

_____

_____

_____

_____

The Committal Service (See p. 41.)

Date_____   Time_____

Location_____

Cemetery address/directions

_____

_____

_____

_____

Plot location_____

The Gathering or Reception (See p. 42 .)

Date_____   Time_____

Location_____

Food

_____

_____

_____

Memory displays

_____

_____

_____

_____

Other details

_____

_____

_____

_____

About the Author

Author, educator and grief counselor Dr. Alan Wolfelt is known across North America for his compassionate messages about healing in grief. He is founder and Director of the Center for Loss and Life Transition in Fort Collins, Colorado. Past recipient of the Association for Death Education and Counseling's Death Educator Award, he is also a faculty member of the University of Colorado Medical School's Department of Family Medicine.

ALSO BY ALAN WOLFELT

Understanding Your Grief
Ten Essential Touchstones for Finding Hope and Healing Your Heart

One of North America's leading grief educators, Dr. Alan Wolfelt has written many books about healing in grief. This book is his most comprehensive, covering the essential lessons that mourners have taught him in his three decades of working with the bereaved.

In compassionate, down-to-earth language, *Understanding Your Grief* describes ten touchstones—or trail markers—that are essential physical, emotional, cognitive, social, and spiritual signs for mourners to look for on their journey through grief.

The Ten Essential Touchstones:

1. Open to the presence of your loss.
2. Dispel misconceptions about grief.
3. Embrace the uniqueness of your grief.
4. Explore what you might experience.
5. Recognize you are not crazy.
6. Understand the six needs of mourning.
7. Nurture yourself.
8. Reach out for help.
9. Seek reconciliation, not resolution.
10. Appreciate your transformation.

Think of your grief as a wilderness—a vast, inhospitable forest. You must journey through this wilderness. To find your way out, you must become acquainted with its terrain and learn to follow the sometimes hard-to-find trail that leads to healing. In the wilderness of your grief, the touchstones are your trail markers. They are the signs that let you know you are on the right path. When you learn to identify and rely on the touchstones, you will find your way to hope and healing.

ISBN 978-1-879651-35-7 • 176 pages • softcover • $14.95

Companion
PRESS

All Dr. Wolfelt's publications can be ordered by mail from:
Companion Press
3735 Broken Bow Road
Fort Collins, CO 80526
(970) 226-6050
www.centerforloss.com

ALSO BY ALAN WOLFELT

The Understanding Your Grief Journal

Exploring the Ten Essential Touchstones

Writing can be a very effective form of mourning, or expressing your grief outside yourself. And it is through mourning that you heal in grief.

The Understanding Your Grief Journal is a companion workbook to Dr. Wolfelt's *Understanding Your Grief*. Designed to help mourners explore the many facets of their unique grief through journaling, this compassionate book interfaces with the ten essential touchstones. Throughout, journalers are asked specific questions about their own unique grief journeys as they relate to the touchstones and are provided with writing space for the many questions asked.

Purchased as a set together with *Understanding Your Grief*, this journal is a wonderful mourning tool and safe place for those in grief. It also makes an ideal grief support group workbook.

ISBN 978-1-879651-39-5 • 150 pages • softcover • $14.95

Companion
PRESS

All Dr. Wolfelt's publications can be ordered by mail from:
Companion Press
3735 Broken Bow Road
Fort Collins, CO 80526
(970) 226-6050
www.centerforloss.com

ALSO BY ALAN WOLFELT

The Wilderness of Grief

Finding Your Way

A beautiful, hardcover gift book version of *Understanding Your Grief*

Understanding Your Grief provides a comprehensive exploration of grief and the ten essential touchstones for finding hope and healing your heart. *The Wilderness of Grief* is an excerpted version of *Understanding Your Grief*, making it approachable and appropriate for all mourners.

This concise book makes an excellent gift for anyone in mourning. On the book's inside front cover is room for writing an inscription to your grieving friend.

While some readers will appreciate the more in-depth *Understanding Your Grief*, others may feel overwhelmed by the amount of information it contains. For these readers we recommend *The Wilderness of Grief*. (Fans of *Understanding Your Grief* will also want a copy of *The Wilderness of Grief* to turn to in spare moments.)

The Wilderness of Grief is an ideal book for the bedside or coffee table. Pick it up before bed and read just a few pages. You'll be carried off to sleep by its gentle, affirming messages of hope and healing.

ISBN 978-1-879651-52-4 • 128 pages • hardcover • $15.95

Companion
PRESS

All Dr. Wolfelt's publications can be ordered by mail from:
Companion Press
3735 Broken Bow Road
Fort Collins, CO 80526
(970) 226-6050
www.centerforloss.com

ALSO BY ALAN WOLFELT

Living in the Shadow of the Ghosts of Grief
Step into the Light

Reconcile old losses and open the
door to infinite joy and love

"Accumulated, unreconciled loss affects every aspect of our lives.
Living in the Shadow *is a beautifully written compass with the*
needle ever-pointing in the direction of hope."
— Greg Yoder, grief counselor

"So often we try to dance around our grief. This book offers the reader a safe place
to do the healing work of "catch-up" mourning, opening the door to a life of freedom,
authenticity and purpose."
— Kim Farris-Luke, bereavement coordinator

Are you depressed? Anxious? Angry? Do you have trouble with trust and intimacy?
Do you feel a lack of meaning and purpose in your life? You may well be living in the
shadow of the ghosts of grief.

When you suffer a loss of any kind—whether through abuse, divorce, job loss, the death
of someone loved or other transitions, you naturally grieve inside. To heal your grief,
you must express it. That is, you must mourn your grief. If you don't, you will carry
your grief into your future, and it will undermine your happiness for the rest of your life.

This compassionate guide will help you learn to identify and mourn your carried grief so
you can go on to live the joyful, whole life you deserve.

ISBN 978-1-879651-51-7 • 160 pages • softcover • $13.95

Companion

All Dr. Wolfelt's publications can be ordered by mail from:
Companion Press
3735 Broken Bow Road
Fort Collins, CO 80526
(970) 226-6050
www.centerforloss.com

ALSO BY ALAN WOLFELT

Healing Your Grieving Heart

100 Practical Ideas

This flagship title in our 100 Ideas Series offers 100 practical ideas to help you practice self-compassion. Some of the ideas teach you the principles of grief and mourning.

The remainder offer practical, action-oriented tips for embracing your grief. Each idea also suggests a carpe diem, which will help you seize the day by helping you move toward your healing today.

ISBN 978-1-879651-25-8 • 128 pages • softcover • $11.95

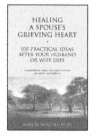

Healing A Spouse's Grieving Heart

100 Practical Ideas After Your Husband or Wife Dies

When your spouse dies, your loss is profound. Not only have you lost the companionship of someone you deeply loved, you have lost the person who shared your history, your helpmate, your lover, perhaps your financial provider.

ISBN 978-1-879651-37-1 • 128 pages • softcover • $11.95

Healing A Child's Grieving Heart

100 Practical Ideas for Families, Friends and Caregivers

Some of the ideas teach about children's unique mourning styles and needs. Others suggest simple activities and "companioning" tips. A compassionate, easy-to-read resource for parents, aunts and uncles, grandparents, teachers, volunteers—and a great refresher for professional caregivers.

ISBN 978-1-879651-28-9 • 128 pages • softcover • $11.95

Companion
PRESS

All Dr. Wolfelt's publications can be ordered by mail from:
Companion Press
3735 Broken Bow Road
Fort Collins, CO 80526
(970) 226-6050
www.centerforloss.com

ALSO BY ALAN WOLFELT

Eight Critical Questions
for Mourners…

And the Answers That Will Help You Heal

When loss enters your life, you are faced with many choices. The questions you ask and the choices you make will determine whether you become among the "living dead" or go on to live until you die. If you are going to integrate grief into your life, it helps to recognize what questions to ask yourself on the journey.

This book provides the answers that will help you clarify your experiences and encourage you to make choices that honor the transformational nature of grief and loss.

ISBN 978-1-879651-62-3 • 176 pages • softcover • $18.95

Understanding Your Suicide Grief

Using the metaphor of the wilderness, Dr. Wolfelt introduces ten Touchstones that will assist the survivor in what is often a complicated grief journey. Learning to identify and rely on the Touchstones helps those touched by suicide find their way to hope and healing.

ISBN 978-1-879651-58-6 • 194 pages • softcover • $14.95

Companion
P R E S S

All Dr. Wolfelt's publications can be ordered by mail from:
Companion Press
3735 Broken Bow Road
Fort Collins, CO 80526
(970) 226-6050
www.centerforloss.com